YOUTH
PROTECTION

How to Protect Your Children From Child Abuse:
A Parent's Guide

D1202517

 BOY SCOUTS OF AMERICA

DEAR PARENT

The Boy Scouts of America is pleased to provide this booklet—it might be the most important information you, your child, and your family will ever read. Understanding these pages could prevent your child or another child from being abused or may empower you to stop abuse as soon as possible and seek the necessary help.

Child abuse is something we would rather not talk about, or even think about, but we must. Every offender benefits from our ignorance. If we fail to do everything we can to keep our children safe, the consequences can be devastating, even deadly.

This booklet cannot address all threats to personal safety your child may experience in and out of Scouting, but it will teach you how to identify and prevent numerous forms of abuse. It contains exercises, based on a set of personal safety rules, that will empower your child to better recognize, respond to, and report abuse. Go through the exercises together. **Your child is that important**. In fact, all children are that important. **Youth Protection Begins With YOU**.

Using This Booklet

This booklet is divided into two sections. The first section contains information for parents about child abuse and some tips for talking with your child about child abuse. The second section contains exercises for you to share with your child. Research shows that children whose parents talk to them about preventing abuse are better able to protect themselves and are more likely to tell if they are abused.

As your child grows, look for opportunities to continue a dialogue about personal safety awareness. Open communication gives children the reassurance that no matter how frightening something may be, their parents are there to help.

WHAT EVERY PARENT SHOULD KNOW

Children can experience abuse in many ways: neglect, physical abuse, sexual abuse, or emotional abuse. Often a child who is abused in one way is abused in multiple ways. When we protect a child from one form of abuse, such as physical abuse, we are often protecting the child from additional forms of abuse.

Neglect

Neglect often involves depriving a child of food, clothing, shelter, medical care, or other necessities of life. Neglect can also involve exposing a child to harmful substances or materials such as drugs, alcohol, or pornography, or to harmful practices such as violent behavior.

> Parents who cannot provide for children as a result of poverty are not committing neglect. Neglect is a deliberate act or inaction that has a physical and emotional impact on a child and, in some instances, can cost a child his life.

A number of clues suggest that a child might be neglected. The child who frequently comes to meetings with body odor, the child who is frequently unkempt, the child who is living in a dangerous environment, and the child with an obvious medical need that goes unattended all are exhibiting signs of potential neglect. So is the child who is always hungry or who hoards or steals food, the child who is seldom dressed appropriately for the weather, and the child who regularly talks of seeing a parent drunk or bruised from being hit.

Any time a child exhibits a need or condition that a reasonable parent would attend to—especially when the failure to provide the need impairs the child's physical or emotional well-being—the child is likely being neglected.

Physical Abuse

Physical abuse is the deliberate injury of a child by a person responsible for the child's care.

Physical abuse injuries can include bruises, broken bones, burns, and abrasions. Children experience minor injuries as a normal part of childhood, usually in places such as the shins, knees, and elbows. When injuries are found in the soft-tissue areas on the abdomen or back, or when they do not seem to be typical childhood injuries, it is possible that the child has been abused.

Blows to the stomach may result in abdominal bruises, even if there is not a visible mark. When a child complains of pain or indicates he was punched in the stomach, such a complaint should be taken seriously, given the possibility of internal injury.

The following signs are commonly associated with abuse but are not absolutes.

- Injuries the child or parent cannot adequately explain
- Injuries on a child who has been absent
- Complaints of soreness when moving
- Fear of going home with or to parents

Talking to Youth About Suspicious Injuries

It is appropriate to ask a child about suspicious injuries. If the child tells of abuse or gives an answer that does not make sense given the location or extent of injuries, you should document this statement and immediately contact the local law enforcement agency or state department of children and family services.

For more information about reporting requirements, call 911 or see the Child Welfare Information Gateway website at www.childwelfare.gov for your state hotline number.

Sexual Abuse

When an adult or older youth uses his or her authority to involve a child in sexual activity, it is child sexual abuse. Sexual abuse includes any activity performed for the sexual satisfaction of the offender. Children can be at risk of sexual abuse anywhere: at home; at a neighbor's house; at school, field trips, and public events; and in Scouting.

A common misconception about sexual abuse is that children are most likely to be abused by strangers. In fact, a sex offender is usually someone the child knows and trusts. Sex offenders are most often male, but females are the offenders in about one-fifth of the incidents involving boys under the age of 14.

Sexual Abuse by Adults

Adults who abuse children may manipulate, bribe, coerce, threaten, or force a child into feeling like a partner in the sexual activity. However, they most often use a multistep "grooming" process that focuses on the child's needs and possibly on the child's parents as well. The sex offender might offer the parents free babysitting services, for example, or make friends with them to gain enough trust to be alone with the child.

Characteristically, the grooming process with the child begins with seemingly harmless touching, such as hugging, massages, exposure, and questionable touching. The sex offender usually seeks a child who craves affection or attention and makes that child feel special by spending a lot of time with him or her and giving gifts and money. But all young children are vulnerable to sexual abuse because of their innocence and total trust in and dependence upon adults.

A red flag may be a person who does not take BSA Youth Protection policies seriously or who exhibits a nonchalant attitude when questioned about an unusual situation.

When the sex offender senses that the child has been sufficiently conditioned to physical contact and has an emotional bond, the physical contact becomes more intrusive. The offender may prey on the child's emerging curiosity about sexuality and may carry on under the guise of sex education or playing inappropriate games. It may involve violating rules, drinking alcohol, smoking cigarettes— all to create a "special relationship."

Most children do not understand that what is happening is sexual or is wrong until it is too late.

Many offenders are clever enough to manipulate the child into believing that he or she is equally to blame or will not be believed if they tell. Many children feel trapped and are afraid to tell.

Sexual Abuse by Other Youth
It is also possible for a child of the same age to abuse another through force or manipulation. About a third of sexual abuse occurs at the hands of other children, including older youth and youth in positions to manipulate through bullying behavior using their size or knowledge difference. Any peer activity, such as a club initiation, in which sexual activity is included is a form of sexual abuse. Overnight activities pose a greater risk of abuse. Personal safety awareness rules should be reviewed before these activities. Adults who learn or discover that youth-on-youth abuse has occurred must take immediate steps to stop it.

Emotional Abuse
A child suffers from emotional abuse when continually ridiculed, blamed, humiliated, or compared unfavorably with others. Emotional abuse damages the child's self-esteem. Studies find that emotional abuse is just as harmful, if not more harmful, than other forms of maltreatment. It can lead to developmental problems, speech delays, depression, anxiety, and conditions such as low empathy and difficulty with peers.

Emotional abuse can occur when a parent completely ignores or rejects or regularly threatens to beat a child or when a child struggles to meet a parent's unreasonable expectations in academics, athletics, or other areas. Emotional abuse can also result if an adult or older youth provides a child with alcohol, drugs, pornography, or other harmful substances or materials.

Spiritual Abuse
An often-overlooked form of child maltreatment is spiritual abuse— the incorporation of religion into the abuse of a child. Some studies suggest that sex offenders are particularly attracted to faith

communities because they find clergy and other faith leaders to be overly trusting. If your child is active in a faith community, make sure it has rigorous child protection policies in place.

Bullying

Bullying is an intentional, aggressive behavior, often involving an imbalance of power or strength, that usually is repeated over a period of time. Bullying can take many forms, including hitting or punching, teasing or name calling, intimidating use of gestures or social exclusion, or sending insulting messages by phone or computer (cyberbullying). Victims of bullying behavior are more likely to be depressed, have low self-esteem, be absent from school or other activities, feel sick, or think about suicide.

Any information indicating a youth has mentioned or talked about suicide must be taken seriously and reported to a responsible leader, law enforcement, or suicide hotline. If your child is being targeted, do not blame your child or tell him or her to ignore the behavior or engage in physical retaliation. Instead, listen carefully and report the bullying behavior to the people

responsible for the program where bullying is occurring. For more information, please see the BSA's Bullying Awareness Web page at www.scouting.org/Training/YouthProtection/bullying.aspx.

Internet/Social Media Safety

Parents play a critical role in keeping children safe from those who use the Internet and social media to access and harm children. Parents can limit the danger by setting basic guidelines such as when children go online, what sites they can visit, and regular check-ins to see and discuss the choices that are being made with technology.

Today's youth are spending more time than ever using digital media for education, research, socializing, and fun. To help families and volunteers keep youth safe while online, the BSA introduced the Cyber Chip. In developing this new tool, the BSA teamed up with content expert NetSmartz®, part of the National Center for Missing and Exploited Children® and training expert for many law enforcement agencies. Earning the Cyber Chip is a requirement for all Cub Scout ranks except Bobcat. For more information, please see the BSA's Cyber Chip Web page at www. scouting.org/Training/YouthProtection/CyberChip.aspx and NCMEC's Netsmartz website at www.netsmartz.org.

Youth With Developmental Disabilities

Children with disabilities or behavioral problems are at greater risk of abuse than other children simply because offenders often target children they believe will be least likely to report abuse. Accordingly, while it is important to teach all children to recognize would-be abusers and to tell a trusted adult about abuse, this message is particularly important for children with disabilities.

Signs Your Child Might Have Been Abused

The best indicator of abuse is a disclosure by your child that someone hurt or scared him or her, or made him or her feel uncomfortable. Unfortunately, many children never speak of abuse, so it is important for you to have ongoing conversations with your child about personal safety and to give repeated reminders that he or she can tell you anything.

Each child's response to abuse is unique. Signs of stress frequently accompany maltreatment, but stress can have many causes. Other possible indicators of abuse include

- Sudden withdrawal from activities the child previously enjoyed
- Reluctance to be around a particular individual, especially in the absence of others
- Changes in behavior or in school performance, including lower grades
- Inability to focus or learning problems with no known cause
- Hypervigilance (excessive watchfulness as if anticipating something bad happening)
- Overly compliant behavior or an excessive desire to please

In addition, a child being sexually victimized may

- Have difficulty sitting or walking
- Complain of pain or itching in the genital or anal areas
- Use sexually explicit language or act out sexual behavior inappropriate for his age

---

If your child is abused by a parent, relative, sibling, or someone else close to you, it may be particularly difficult for him or her to disclose abuse to you and also difficult for you to accept. Studies show that children rarely lie about sexual abuse or other maltreatment. Accordingly, if your child discloses abuse or even expresses discomfort with a particular person or situation, always take that as your cue to act. Children communicate with us through their language, their behaviors, and their emotions. Communication about abuse is often subtle and indirect. A child may offer a disguised disclosure, saying something like, "I have a friend who ...," in an attempt to gauge how an adult will react. The child who receives a helpful or sympathetic response is more likely to disclose any abuse experiences.

Speaking With a Child Who Discloses or Indicates Abuse

When speaking with a child who discloses or indicates abuse, your role is to become the trusted adult. A good approach includes the following.

- Be an upstander; get involved.
- If you see something, stop it.
- If you know or suspect something, report it.
- If you are not sure, seek advice from an expert.

If a child does disclose abuse, it is important that adults respond calmly and in a supportive manner. Avoid statements that might indicate shame, blame, disbelief, disgust, or fear. If the abuse started or occurred much earlier, avoid asking a child why he did not tell anyone sooner. Tell the child it wasn't his or her fault, and express belief in the child's disclosure by simply stating, "I believe you." This will further support and validate the child's statement. Avoid asking children for detailed information. Ask basic, open-ended questions to discern the following information:

- Name and address of the alleged victim, if known
- Name and address of the alleged offender, if known
- Location of the alleged abuse
- Nature (e.g., sexual, physical, emotional) and extent of the alleged abuse
- Approximate date of the last incident (if an older child)

Adults should recognize that talking with children about maltreatment, especially sexual abuse, is not natural or comfortable for anyone; however, a child's first disclosure—and your response—may have lasting effects. If the child senses you do not want to hear about his or her experiences or senses that he or she is saying something wrong, the child might shut down. Simply let the child know that you believe him or her, you care, it wasn't his or her fault, and you want to help.

The BSA's Barriers to Abuse

You should expect your child's Cub Scout pack to follow the Youth Protection policies put in place by the BSA to provide additional safety for your child and all who are involved in Scouting. These policies also protect adult leaders from the rare possibility of a false report. Scout leaders who are in positions of youth leadership and supervision outside of the Scouting program should follow these practices in those roles as well.

Two-deep leadership on all trips and outings is required.
A minimum of two registered adult leaders, or one registered leader and a parent of a participating Scout or another adult, one of whom must be 21 years of age or older, is required for any Scouting trips and outings. All youth need to know that adults are there if needed.

The policy of two-deep leadership extends into cyberspace.
There should be no one-on-one online or digital activities (games, social media, etc.) or electronic communications. Leaders should include or copy a parent or another adult leader in all online communications, ensuring no one-on-one contact exists in text, social media, or other forms of online or digital communication.

One-on-one contact between adults and youth is prohibited.
In situations requiring a personal conference, the meeting is to be conducted with the knowledge and in view of other adults and youth.

Separate accommodations for adults and youth are required. When camping, no youth is permitted to sleep in the tent of an adult other than his or her own parent or legal guardian. Councils should have separate shower and latrine facilities for adults and youth as well as females. When separate facilities are not available, separate times for male and female showers should be scheduled and posted. Likewise, youth and adults must shower at different times.

The buddy system should be used at all times. The buddy system is a safety measure for all Scouting activities. Buddies should be known to each other, self-selected, and of the same approximate age and experience level. The buddy system in Scouting has shown it is always best to have another person with you when involved in any outdoor or strenuous activity. If needed, a buddy team may consist of three Scouts. No youth should ever be forced into or made to feel uncomfortable by a buddy assignment.

Privacy of youth is respected. All youth and adult leaders must respect the privacy of youth in situations such as changing clothes and taking showers at camp. Adults may enter youth changing or showering areas only to the extent that health and safety requires. Adults must protect their own privacy in similar situations.

Inappropriate use of smartphones, cameras, or imaging or digital devices is prohibited. Although most Scouts and leaders use cameras and other imaging devices responsibly, it has become very easy to invade the privacy of individuals. It is inappropriate to use any device capable of recording or transmitting visual images in shower houses, restrooms, or other areas where privacy is expected.

No secret organizations allowed. The BSA does not recognize any secret organization as part of its program. All aspects of the Scouting program are open to observation by parents and leaders.

No hazing. Physical hazing and initiations are prohibited and may not be included as part of any Scouting activity.

No bullying. Verbal, physical, and cyber bullying are prohibited in Scouting.

Youth leadership is monitored by adult leaders. Adult leaders must monitor and guide the leadership techniques used by youth leaders and ensure that BSA policies are followed.

Discipline must be constructive. Discipline used in Scouting should be constructive and reflect Scouting's values. Corporal punishment is never permitted. Disciplinary activities involving isolation, humiliation, or ridicule are prohibited. Examples of positive discipline include verbal praise and high fives.

Appropriate attire is required for all activities. Proper clothing for activities is required. For example, skinny-dipping or revealing bathing suits are not appropriate in Scouting.

All adult leaders and youth members have responsibility. Everyone is responsible for acting in accordance with the Scout Oath and Scout Law. Physical violence, sexual activity, emotional abuse, spiritual abuse, unauthorized weapons, hazing, discrimination, initiation rites, bullying, cyberbullying, theft, verbal insults, drugs, alcohol, or pornography have no place in the Scouting program and may result in revocation of membership. For more information, please see the BSA's *Guide to Safe Scouting* and other Youth Protection resources.

Reporting Child Abuse and Violations of Policies

All persons involved in Scouting have two required procedures for reporting Youth Protection–related incidents.

Mandatory Report of Child Abuse. All persons involved in Scouting shall report to local law enforcement any good-faith suspicion or belief that any child is or has been physically or sexually abused, physically or emotionally neglected, exposed to any form of violence or threat, or exposed to any form of sexual exploitation, including the possession, manufacture, or distribution of child pornography, online solicitation, enticement, or showing of obscene material. No person may abdicate this reporting responsibility to any other person. For more information, please see your state's reporting statutes on the Child Welfare Information Gateway website at www.childwelfare.gov/systemwide/laws_policies/state/.

Parents Reporting Violations of BSA Youth Protection Policies. If you have reason to believe any of the BSA's Youth Protection policies have been violated, including mandatory reporting of abuse of a child, you must notify your Scout executive so he or she may take appropriate action for the safety of our Scouts.

If a Scoutmaster or someone else in Scouting is trying to convince your child that merit badges or other advancement are solely dependent on his or her approval, or if he or she is asking your child to do anything that seems inappropriate, please immediately contact your Scout executive.

Scouting-Required Steps to Reporting Child Abuse*

1. Ensure the child is in a safe environment.
2. In cases of child abuse or medical emergencies, call 911 immediately. In addition, if the suspected abuse is in the Scout's home or family, you are required to contact the local child protective services office.
3. Notify the Scout executive, or the executive's designee during his or her absence. (Contact names and telephone numbers can be found using the BSA local council locator at www.scouting.org/LocalCouncilLocator.aspx.)

*State laws may vary.

Consider having a "Family Safety Night" at the beginning and the end of every school year or new activity. Reviewing rules about bike helmets, fire escape plans, and calling 911 should lead into conversations about personal safety awareness and online safety so that they can be treated like any other concern.

EXERCISES ON PERSONAL SAFETY AWARENESS

Now that you understand the scope of the problem and how the BSA is working to keep children safe, let us focus on helping you empower your child. Concerned and connected caregivers are a strong component of all child abuse prevention strategies. You have an important role to play in prevention!

Many parents find it difficult to talk with their child about abuse. However, it is important to provide a foundation for a child to understand body ownership and encouragement to come to you with questions and concerns. The personal safety exercises in this section, to be used in conversations with your child, will help you with this process.

Five Topics to Cover With Children

NOTE: Completing the exercises described within these pages fulfills the requirements for your son to earn his badge or rank and must be completed for each rank he earns.

Network of Trusted Adults

Young people should have at least five adults you have identified to whom they can talk freely about their feelings and problems and who provide healthy attention and affection. A child who has such a network of trusted adults will be more difficult for a sex offender to groom. The list of five adults might change depending on the child's circumstances. Prior to Scouting or other activities, parents should discuss with their child who he or she will turn to if someone is violating a rule or making them uncomfortable.

Try this exercise to help your child identify trusted adults. Explain that a trusted adult is someone he or she knows well who is willing to listen and offer advice when needed. Trace your child's hand on a piece of paper. Ask your child to write or draw a person on each finger that he or she can go to for help or advice. Help your child determine the trusted adults. Explain that if a situation occurs where a trusted adult is needed, he or she needs to remember this list. And if one of the people on the list cannot help, or is the one causing the problem, he or she should go to another.

Ask your child these questions, making sure the options are understood (samples responses are given).

"What if something happens on a camping trip (or at a neighbor's house, or at a friend's house) that makes you feel afraid or confused?" I could talk to my pack leader about it right away. He said we could talk to him about anything that made us feel unsafe. When I get home, I would tell a parent what happened.

"What if someone is making you feel unsafe, and the first person you tell can't help you?" I would tell one of my other trusted grown-ups until I find one who can help.

"What if one of your trusted adults is making you feel unsafe or uncomfortable?" I am allowed to say NO to any adult who makes me feel afraid, confused, or unsafe. I would say NO and then contact one of the other adults on my list to get help.

Check First

Many abusers are known to the child as a family friend, relative, or older youth, so it is important to focus safety messages on the behavior of a person, not the relationship to the child. Teach your child to check with you first before agreeing to go anywhere with another person. Tell your child never to go anywhere with anyone who will not let him or her check with you first. If the person refuses, your child has the right to step back from the person, make noise, run away, and tell someone.

Tell your child that your permission is required before he or she may accept an invitation from a Scout leader or another parent to an activity outside of Scouting and that all such invitations must be reported to you. The BSA recommends that parents insist that two adults are present (two-deep leadership) when authorizing non-Scouting activities for their children.

Try this exercise to help your child remember to check first. Brainstorm times and situations in which your child should always come to you before going somewhere with someone. Include such situations as going into a house or vehicle, changing plans, being offered gifts, and being asked for help.

Talk through scenarios like the following.

"What if a neighbor asks you to come into his house to see his new puppy?" I would tell him that I need to check with you first. I would come home and check first before I went over to their house.

"What if you are playing in the park and a nice person asks you to come to a different part of the park to help him or her find something they lost?" I need to check first before changing my plans so that my parents know where I am. I also need to check first before helping an adult. Adults usually ask other adults for help. I can help if I check first and you come with me to ask my parents for permission.

Trust Your Gut Instinct—The "Uh-Oh" Feeling

Animals and humans have a gut instinct that helps keep us safe. Teach your child to listen to that "uh-oh" feeling that might occur if your child is in a place that does not feel right or with a person who is making him or her feel confused or scared. Encourage your child to go to a trusted adult if the "uh-oh" feeling starts.

Try this exercise to help your child learn to trust his or her gut instinct. Tell your child that any time someone makes his or her uh-oh feeling start, he or she has your permission to take some big steps back and say "NO," and then go tell a trusted adult what happened. Explain that stepping back can give him or her room to think and move. Then have your child practice taking big steps away from a person and saying "NO" in a firm voice.

Discuss the following situation with your child.

"What if someone drives up, gets out of their car, and starts walking toward you to ask you for directions?" My uh-oh alarm might go off, because I know adults should ask adults for help. I know I would need to check first. So I would start moving away from the person, say that I have to check first, and go quickly to the person taking care of me.

Secrets and Surprises

Sex offenders often try to groom children by convincing them to keep secrets about activities that they would not want their parents to know about (drinking, smoking, pornography, etc.). If the child wants to keep those activities secret, he or she might also see any abuse as something to keep secret. Your child must feel like he or she can come to you and be heard about little concerns as well as big problems. Tell your child it is not OK for people to ask him or her to keep a secret from you or another caregiver. Give your child a simple, automatic solution. Let your child know that he or she can come to you about anything and that you will still love and support him or her.

Try this exercise to help your child discern the difference between secrets and surprises. Tell your child that a secret is something that is hidden from others. A surprise is something that we keep quiet about for a short period of time and then everyone finds out together, like what you bought someone for his or her birthday. Surprises are usually OK, but secrets can be harmful if they cover up something unsafe or scary. Tell your child that if he or she is not sure that something is a secret or a surprise, he or she can always ask you or a trusted adult.

Ask your child what to do in the following situations.

"What if a bigger kid says he will give you $5 if you play a secret touching game with him?" My uh-oh alarm would probably go off, because that is against our family rules. I would take a few steps back, so I had room to think, and say NO in a strong voice. I would tell a trusted adult what happened.

"What if someone you know asks if he can email you a secret picture?" I would tell him that I don't want him to send it. If he sends it anyway, I would check with you first before opening the email. (For additional information, please see the BSA's Cyber Chip tool and resources at www.scouting.org/Training/YouthProtection/CyberChip.aspx and the NetSmartz Scouting Portal at www.netsmartz.org/scouting.)

Talk About Touches and Private Parts

Young people should be told that the parts of their body covered by their swimsuit are their private parts and they have the right to say no to being touched there. Body parts should be called by their appropriate names to assist in developing a healthy and positive body image. Encourage your child to say no and then tell you if someone tries to touch or look at his or her private parts or wants him or her to touch or look at their private parts.

It is important to remind children that if they get tricked into a scary or confusing touch or if they freeze and are unable to say no, it is OK and not their fault. Children should be encouraged to tell as soon as they feel comfortable doing so. Keep the lines of communication open by reminding them that they can talk to you about touches, even a long time after something happened.

Try this exercise to help your child resist someone who is trying to touch his or her private parts. Pose these scenarios with him or her, and then discuss the solutions.

"What if your friend's babysitter or another youth asks you to wrestle without clothes on?" I know that I am allowed to say NO to anyone asking me to do private part touches. I would take a few steps back so I have room to think, say NO in a strong voice, and head home.

"What if that same friend asks you to keep the touching games secret?" That would probably make my uh-oh alarm go off, because we don't keep secrets. I would let my friend know that what happened isn't his fault, and I would still come and tell you.

Putting It Together

Reviewing these five personal safety rules and allowing your child to design his or her own "What If" games can help make personal safety awareness less scary and more accessible for your child and the whole family. The most important points to make sure your child knows are as follows:

- Form a net.
- Check first.
- Trust your gut.
- Avoid secrets.
- Talk about touches.

ADDITIONAL RESOURCES

The *Guide to Safe Scouting* exists to help members of the BSA conduct Scouting activities in a safe and prudent manner. It can be accessed online at http://www.scouting.org/scoutsource/HealthandSafety/GSS.aspx.

Find your nearest BSA local council using scouting.org's **Local Council Locator** feature at http://www.scouting.org/localcouncillocator.aspx.

The **National Council's Youth Protection Team** can be contacted by email at Youth.Protection@scouting.org or by telephone at 972-580-2000.

BSA Youth Protection Materials

Along with this booklet, the Boy Scouts of America has an educational video for use by Cub Scout packs or dens. This award-winning production provides age-appropriate information about sexual abuse of boys.

"It Happened to Me" is a video for Cub Scout–age boys that portrays common situations in which sexual abuse can occur. The video discusses how sex offenders often resort to tricks for gaining access to their victims. It emphasizes that if a boy is sexually abused, he should talk to his parents or other trusted adults. The video also stresses that it is not the child's fault if he is sexually abused; it is the sex offender who is responsible. "It Happened to Me" is available from your local BSA council and should be shown to boys 6 to 10 years of age only when a parent or other adult family member is present with the child. The BSA encourages the video to be viewed by each Cub Scout pack or den annually. Meeting guides in both English and Spanish can be found online at www.scouting.org/training/youthprotection/cubscout.aspx.

To help families and volunteers keep youth safe while online, the BSA introduced the **Cyber Chip** in conjunction with NetSmartz®. The material is tailored at each grade level for age-appropriateness. Go to www.scouting.org/cyberchip.

For Scouting's leaders and parents, the BSA has a video training session, **Youth Protection Guidelines: Training for Volunteer Leaders and Parents.** This is available from your BSA local council, with regular training sessions scheduled in most districts.

In addition to the video-based training, **Youth Protection training** is available on the BSA's website at www.scouting.org/Training/YouthProtection.aspx. The training addresses many questions Scouting volunteers and parents have regarding child sexual abuse.

In addition to these video and online materials, the BSA provides Youth Protection information to its members and families through *Boys' Life* and *Scouting* magazines.

For **more information** on Youth Protection, visit www.scouting.org/Training/YouthProtection.aspx.

Recommended Reading
Books for Children
My Body Belongs to Me by Jill Starishevsky (helping children learn about their bodies and assuring children that it is OK to tell)

It's My Body by Lory Freeman (teaching young children what to do about uncomfortable touches)

A Very Touching Book by Jan Hindman (teaching children what to do if there is "secret" touching; introduces and uses correct terms for genitals)

Books for Adults
How to Talk So Kids Will Listen & Listen So Kids Will Talk by Adele Faber and Elaine Mazlish (tested strategies to use for better parent/child communication)

Parents Preventing Abuse by Dr. Jaime Romo (e-book that guides parents to mitigate the conditions that allow child sexual abuse and prevent abuse of their children)

Other Sources of Child Abuse Prevention Information
Gundersen National Child Protection Training Center
Winona State University
Maxwell Hall, 2nd Floor
Winona, MN 55987
Telephone: 507-457-2890
www.gundersenhealth.org/ncptc

Child Welfare Information Gateway
1250 Maryland Ave., SW, 8th Floor
Washington, DC 20024
Telephone: 800-394-3366
info@childwelfare.gov
www.childwelfare.gov

Jacob Wetterling Resource Center
Gundersen National Child Protection Training Center
2021 E. Hennepin Ave., Suite 360
Minneapolis, MN 55413
Telephone: 507-457-2890
www.gundersenhealth.org

National Center for Missing & Exploited Children
699 Prince St.
Alexandria, VA 22314-3175
Telephone: 800-843-5678
www.missingkids.com
www.netsmartz.org

National Children's Advocacy Center
210 Pratt Ave.
Huntsville, Alabama 35801
Telephone: 256-533-KIDS (5437)
www.nationalcac.org

stopbullying.gov
200 Independence Ave., SW
Washington, DC 20201

Acknowledgment

Special thanks to **Gundersen National Child Protection Training Center** for invaluable assistance in the development of this pamphlet.

Prepared. For Life.®

BOY SCOUTS OF AMERICA
1325 West Walnut Hill Lane
P.O. Box 152079
Irving, Texas 75015-2079
www.scouting.org

100-014
2015 Printing